First edition for the United States
and Canada published in 2014
by Barron's Educational Series, Inc.

First published in 2014 by Wayland
Text copyright © Pat Thomas 2014
Illustrations copyright © Wayland 2014

Wayland is a division of Hachette Children's Books,
a Hachette UK company.
www.hachette.co.uk

Concept design: Kate Buxton
Series design: Paul Cherrill for Basement68
Editor: Victoria Brooker

All inquiries should be addressed to:
Barron's Educational Series, Inc.
250 Wireless Boulevard
Hauppauge, New York 11788
www.barronseduc.com

ISBN: 978-1-4380-0479-2

Library of Congress Control Number: 2013957082

Date of manufacture: August 2017
Manufactured by: Wing King Tong Printing Ltd., Guangdong, China

Printed in China

9 8 7 6 5 4

I See Things Differently

A FIRST LOOK AT AUTISM

PAT THOMAS
ILLUSTRATED BY CLAIRE KEAY

BARRON'S

Do you know what it feels like to be worried or nervous or scared – or to feel different from other people?

We all feel these things
sometimes. But people who have
autism feel these things a lot.

You probably know someone with autism. It could be someone at school, or in your neighborhood, or even in your own family.

You may have seen them behaving in ways that seem strange to you, and wondered why they do these things.

But even if you asked them, they might not be able to explain. In fact, some people with autism don't speak at all.

Autism is something you are born
with – it's not something that you
can catch from others.

When people have autism, it affects the way
their brain works, making them behave or react
differently from others.

Nobody knows exactly what causes it,
and figuring that out isn't easy because the
way our brains work is very complicated.

Our brains help us make sense of the world. They help us learn from the things we do and see.

They help us understand that if someone is smiling, that means they are happy.

Or that the green pencil works just as well as the red one.
Or if you put the peanut butter on first and then the jam,
it tastes the same as if you put the jam on first.

What about you?

Do you know someone who has autism?

Can you say what you think autism is?

But for people with autism,
their brain works differently from
other people's.

They may look the same as everyone else on the outside, but inside they can feel like everyone around them is speaking a different language – or from a different planet!

People with autism may find big crowds
or loud noises very frightening.

They may repeat the same words over and over again or move their bodies in ways that look strange to you.

When you talk
to them they may
not look at you,
and you may
wonder if they are
hearing what you say.

Even small changes can be very upsetting to them. That's why they may always want to sit in the same chair, or read the same book, or use the same cup.

These habits help people with autism feel safer and more able to deal with all the things they are feeling.

What about you?

If you know someone with autism, what are some of the habits that make them feel safe? Do you have habits that make you feel safe, too?

Most of us are pretty good at finding ways
to ignore things that we don't want to
see or hear or do.

But for people with autism, it can be
harder to ignore things.

All the sights and sounds and smells
around them come rushing into their brains
like a giant wave. When that happens,
they may feel lots of confusing
feelings all at once.

People with autism aren't bad or behaving wrongly; they are just different.

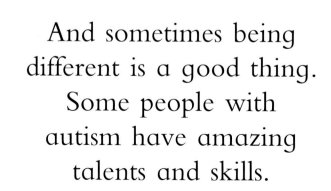

And sometimes being different is a good thing. Some people with autism have amazing talents and skills.

They may be good at music or painting or remembering things. They may be really good at math or understanding computer programs or fixing things.

When people have autism, it can be hard for them to understand jokes or use their imagination or play pretend games.

Being with more than one person at a time may be upsetting, and it could be hard for them to make friends.

But we all need friends to love
and support us. So if you know someone
with autism, try to be a good friend.

Be kind and patient and don't expect him or her to
"grow out of it." That won't happen. He or she
will always see the world a little differently from others.

But with love and support from everyone
around them, people with autism can
learn to feel a little happier
and safer each day.

HOW TO USE THIS BOOK

This book is intended for children who may have siblings with autism, and those who may have classmates with autism. Its aim is to promote understanding by explaining in simple terms what autism is and what it feels like from the perspective of the child with autism. It also acknowledges the difficulties that those who are not autistic sometimes have in understanding those who are.

Tackle myths and misconceptions. Children hear all sorts of things outside the home about what autism is and isn't. Some of this information can be confusing or wrong. Parents and teachers have a crucial role in promoting an understanding of what autism is. To help others understand what autism is like, do your homework, be clear about what autism is, where your child sits on the spectrum, and how other families or classrooms can positively support a child with autism. The better informed you are, the more confident you will feel to field questions.

Keep talking. Children are naturally curious and they want to understand. The questions in the "What about you?" sections can be useful prompts for understanding things from your child's point of view. Use them to begin discussions about autism. Remember, however, that telling doesn't guarantee understanding. With very young children you may have to have this conversation – or read this book with them – more than once.

Find ways for them to help. Siblings and classmates can be a great support – if they know what to do. Find age-appropriate ways of encouraging interaction. It could be help with homework, or just sitting quietly together. Help them learn to feel confident in following, rather than leading, the autistic child's agenda. Remind them to always ask an adult for help if their sibling or classmate with autism becomes agitated.

Go with the flow. Children with autism are not tactful; they may say things that seem hurtful or inappropriate. Help your child to feel confident not to take what their friend or sibling with autism says too seriously or too personally. Children with autism may also like to smell or feel things that seem odd to others. This is just because they have different ways of finding out about other people or new things. Help those around them to understand that this is just how they are.

Manage your time. In families who have a child with autism, it can feel like everything – from story time to meal time – is focussed on understanding the needs of the child with autism. This means that other siblings may not get the attention they need. In addition to doing things as a family, it's also important that you do things separately with your non-autistic child(ren) and help take the burden of being understanding and being on the sidelines off their shoulders for a while. If, for example, there are important events where the non-autistic child should be the center of attention (such as a school play), consider whether it's appropriate for your child with autism to attend. Where possible, parents should take advantage of support from family, extended family, formal support networks, and friends that allows them to have some time off, too.

At school. Talking about autism can help classmates to be more understanding. Invite parents of children with autism to come into class and talk about their experiences and their children, and to answer questions. Many classrooms these days integrate children of all abilities. Discussion helps reinforce the message that we all have things we are good at and things we are not so good at. Reassure students that your job is to help build on the strengths of each child, while encouraging them to develop in areas where they are less strong. Likewise it is never too early to teach children that learning to get along, and finding common ground with those who are different from us, is a vital part of becoming an adult. And that autism is a disability in the same way as a hearing or sight impairment or other physical disability. Autism is sometimes called the hidden disability because you can't see it.

BOOKS TO READ

For children

My Brother Is Autistic (Let's Talk About It!)
Jennifer Moore-Mallinos
(Barron's, 2008)

My Brother Is Different: A Book for Young Children Who Have a Brother or Sister with Autism
Louise Gorrod
(National Autistic Society, 2000)

A Friend Like Simon
Kate Gaynot
(Special Stories, 2008)

Looking After Louis
Lesley Ely
(Frances Lincoln Children's Books, 2005)

For parents and older children

Everybody Is Different: A Book for Young People Who Have Brothers or Sisters with Autism
Fiona Bleach
(National Autism Society, 2001)

Different Like Me: My Book of Autism Heroes
Marc Thomas
(Jessica Kingsley Publishers, 2005)

101 Games and Activities for Children with Autism, Asperger's, and Sensory Processing Disorders
Tara Delaney
(McGraw-Hill Contemporary, 2009)

RESOURCES FOR ADULTS

U.S. Autism and Asperger's Association
usautism.org

National Autism Association
http://nationalautismassociation.org

The Puzzle of Autism
www.nea.org/assets/docs/HE/autismpuzzle.pdf
A downloadable education guide produced by the National Education Association. This publication explores many of the characteristics of autism and give strategies for addressing them in the classroom.